F

by Andrew Fergusson

Lang**Syne**

PUBLISHING

WRITING *to* REMEMBER

Lang**Syne**

PUBLISHING

WRITING *to* REMEMBER

79 Main Street, Newtongrange,
Midlothian EH22 4NA
Tel: 0131 344 0414   Fax: 0845 075 6085
E-mail: info@lang-syne.co.uk
www.langsyneshop.co.uk

Design by Dorothy Meikle
Printed by Printwell Ltd
© Lang Syne Publishers Ltd 2018

ISBN 978-1-85217-043-1

Fergusson

SEPT NAMES INCLUDE:

Fergie
Fergus
Ferries
Forgie
Keddie
Kiddie
MacAdie
MacFergus
MacKeddie
MacKerras
MacKersey

Fergusson

MOTTO:
Sweeter after difficulty.

CREST:
A bee on a thistle.

TERRITORY:
Argyll, Dumfries and Galloway.

Chapter one:

The origins of the clan system

by Rennie McOwan

The original Scottish clans of the Highlands and the great families of the Lowlands and Borders were gatherings of families, relatives, allies and neighbours for mutual protection against rivals or invaders.

Scotland experienced invasion from the Vikings, the Romans and English armies from the south. The Norman invasion of what is now England also had an influence on land-holding in Scotland. Some of these invaders stayed on and in time became 'Scottish'.

The word clan derives from the Gaelic language term 'clann', meaning children, and it was first used many centuries ago as communities were formed around tribal lands in glens and mountain fastnesses.

The format of clans changed over the centuries, but at its best the chief and his family held the land on behalf of all, like trustees, and the ordinary clansmen and women believed they had a blood relationship with the founder of their clan.

There were two way duties and obligations. An inadequate chief could be deposed and replaced by someone of greater ability.

Clan people had an immense pride in race. Their relationship with the chief was like adult children to a father and they had a real dignity.

The concept of clanship is very old and a more feudal notion of authority gradually crept in.

Pictland, for instance, was divided into seven principalities ruled by feudal leaders who were the strongest and most charismatic leaders of their particular groups.

By the sixth century the 'British' kingdoms of Strathclyde, Lothian and Celtic Dalriada (Argyll) had emerged and Scotland, as one nation, began to take shape in the time of King Kenneth MacAlpin.

Some chiefs claimed descent from

ancient kings which may not have been accurate in every case.

By the twelfth and thirteenth centuries the clans and families were more strongly brought under the central control of Scottish monarchs.

Lands were awarded and administered more and more under royal favour, yet the power of the area clan chiefs was still very great.

The long wars to ensure Scotland's independence against the expansionist ideas of English monarchs extended the influence of some clans and reduced the lands of others.

Those who supported Scotland's greatest king, Robert the Bruce, were awarded the territories of the families who had opposed his claim to the Scottish throne.

In the Scottish Borders country – the notorious Debatable Lands – the great families built up a ferocious reputation for providing warlike men accustomed to raiding into England and occasionally fighting one another.

Chiefs had the power to dispense justice and to confiscate lands and clan warfare produced a society where martial virtues – courage, hardiness, tenacity – were greatly admired.

Gradually the relationship between the clans and the Crown became strained as Scottish monarchs became more orientated to life in the Lowlands and, on occasion, towards England.

The Highland clans spoke a different language, Gaelic, whereas the language of Lowland Scotland and the court was Scots and in more modern times, English.

Highlanders dressed differently, had different customs, and their wild mountain land sometimes seemed almost foreign to people living in the Lowlands.

It must be emphasised that Gaelic culture was very rich and story-telling, poetry, piping, the clarsach (harp) and other music all flourished and were greatly respected.

Highland culture was different from other parts of Scotland but it was not inferior or less sophisticated.

Central Government, whether in London or Edinburgh, sometimes saw the Gaelic clans as

*"The spirit of the clan means much
to thousands of people"*

a challenge to their authority and some sent expeditions into the Highlands and west to crush the power of the Lords of the Isles.

Nevertheless, when the eighteenth century Jacobite Risings came along the cause of the Stuarts was mainly supported by Highland clans.

The word Jacobite comes from the Latin for James – Jacobus. The Jacobites wanted to restore the exiled Stuarts to the throne of Britain.

The monarchies of Scotland and England became one in 1603 when King James VI of Scotland (1st of England) gained the English throne after Queen Elizabeth died.

The Union of Parliaments of Scotland and England, the Treaty of Union, took place in 1707.

Some Highland clans, of course, and Lowland families opposed the Jacobites and supported the incoming Hanoverians.

After the Jacobite cause finally went down at Culloden in 1746 a kind of ethnic cleansing took place. The power of the chiefs was curtailed. Tartan and the pipes were banned in law.

Many emigrated, some because they

wanted to, some because they were evicted by force. In addition, many Highlanders left for the cities of the south to seek work.

Many of the clan lands became home to sheep and deer shooting estates.

But the warlike traditions of the clans and the great Lowland and Border families lived on, with their descendants fighting bravely for freedom in two world wars.

Remember the men from whence you came, says the Gaelic proverb, and to that could be added the role of many heroic women.

The spirit of the clan, of having roots, whether Highland or Lowland, means much to thousands of people.

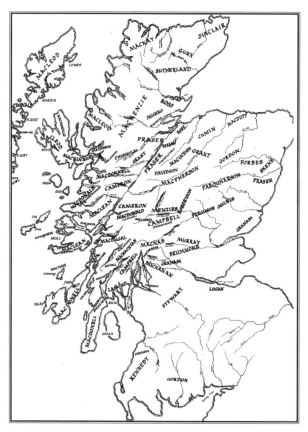

A map of the clans' homelands

Chapter two:

Omen in the sky

The Fergussons are famed for great achievements. The name means simply son of Fergus and was a popular Christian name among the Gaels who crossed from Ulster to Argyll.

Fergus was an Irish chief who settled in Kintyre in the sixth century and brought the Stone of Scone to Scotland, which eventually became the Coronation Stone. It was Fergus who established the kingdom of Dalriada along the West Coast. Fergus itself is a personal appellation in its secondary sense, implying a hero, but primarily signifying a man, said to derive from fear and gias, or geis signifying a spear, the weapon carried by the Gais-gach, or heavy armed warrior among the Highlanders. The Gaelic name is Clan Fhearghuis.

Fergussons lay claim to being responsible for Scotland having the Saltire, the white diagonal cross on a blue background, as her flag.

Angus (Hungas) MacFergus, a Pictish king descended through his mother from the Dalriadic Fergussons, was a great warrior and in the ninth century extended his overlordship for a time from the Shetlands to the Humber. At Athelstaneford, in East Lothian, his army faced a much larger army of the Northumbrians and their allies. Some legends say Fergus had a dream and saw a white Saltire cross in a blue sky, others say his men saw it themselves in the sky. They took it as divine favour and an excellent omen and won a crushing victory.

Angus MacFergus from then on adopted the white cross and blue background as his own flag and it was eventually to become the flag of all Scotland.

Fergus, Prince of Galloway, in the 1160s was founder of the Fergussons of Craigdarroch in Dumfriesshire and on a charter dated 1215 signed himself as Duncan, son of Gilbert, son of Fergus, Prince of Galloway.

Fergus of Galloway was of the old Scots Royal line and married a daughter of Henry the First of England. His grandson, Duncan, became Earl of Carrick and therefore an ancestor of King Robert the Bruce, proof of the royal blood in the veins of the Fergussons who descended from this line.

But what of the other Fergussons in
Ayrshire, Argyll, Atholl and the north-east? Their
origin is uncertain but it seems probable that they
started in Argyll, possibly with King Fergus, and
spread in one wave to Atholl and then to
Aberdeenshire and Fife, whilst another wave went
south to Ayrshire, with the Galloway family
perhaps descended from this line of the branch.

The evidence for this theory includes the
name of the Ayrshire family, Fergussons of
Kilkerran which is said to stem from St Ciaran,
one of the earliest Irish missionary saints to land
in Scotland.

An 18th century manuscript held by the
Aberdeenshire Fergussons records the tradition of
their origins in this way: the two sons of the chief
of the Fergusson in Cowal became involved in an
affray with a neighbouring chief and were forced
to leave the area.

One went to Aberdeenshire, the other to
Ayrshire. This is said to have happened upwards
of 400 years ago.

Also, in Atholl, the universal tradition is

that the clan Fergus and MacDermots of Glen Lyon were the two oldest clans in the district and one Perthshire historian, writing in the 19th century, noted that he had not yet met a Highland Fergusson who did not claim descent from King Fergus.

There are two further reasons for accepting the Fergusson traditions of antiquity and kinship. Their heraldry, uniform from a very early period, was a silver buckle surrounded by three boars heads for the Argyll, Ayrshire and north-eastern branches, and a blue lion rampant for the possibly distinct Galloway line.

It is clear that Fergussons all over Scotland looked to the house of Kilkerran in Ayrshire for their ultimate chief from an early date. In the sixteenth century a Fergusson of Atholl, convicted of a felony at Edinburgh, appealed to Kilkerran for protection and in 1727 two Aberdeenshire branches of the clan called on Kilkerran to mediate in a dispute between them.

Although there were already five separate Fergusson branches at the beginning of their recorded history in the 14th century the bearers of the name have always felt themselves to be related and have been recognised as such by most other Scots.

The Argyll branch settled in Cowal and Kintyre and quite possibly the remnant of the original race looked to them for leadership. The laird was known as the chief of clan Fergus of Strachur and was subject to the Earls of Argyll.

These Fergussons were renowned for their stature and strength and one story to illustrate this reputation is told of a fifteenth century clansman who fell behind with the federal dues he owed to Argyll.

As he saw a posse of Campbells approaching his house one day, obviously intent on collecting the dues by force, he turned to his sons in despair, asking them how they were to defend themselves.

The chief's two sons, like him well over six feet and big with it, told him not to panic and to allow the Campbells to come in unhindered. The two sides met in the laird's orchard and when the Campbells demanded the money and fingered their swords menacingly, the Fergusson brothers simply stepped to one side, wrenched two young trees bodily from the ground, and swung them at their astonished foes fled in terror on seeing such a display of strength.

When the Earl of Argyll heard of this feat he was so impressed that he pardoned the Fergussons from all taxation in return for a promise of military service from the two young strongmen. Perhaps he would have been less excited had he discovered that the brothers had taken the precaution of digging up the tree roots as their foes came up to the house.

The Fife branch of the clan based at Raith was probably descended from a junior line of the Fergussons of Atholl. Although very small in numbers it produced the first Fergusson to rise to national fame – David Fergusson, one of the great ministers of the Protestant reformation.

This man, though apparently without formal education, was ranked second only to John Knox as a preacher and eventually rose to be twice Moderator of the General Assembly of the Church of Scotland.

The Fergussons of Atholl lived mainly along the River Tummel with minor branches to the east and southwest in Strathyre. Gradually they became subject to the Murrays of Atholl as their local landlords though this could often clash with their loyalty to their lowland cousins.

Like the Argyll family they were known for their great height and toughness and they too have a famous legend to back up this reputation. It concerns one of the chiefs of Dunfallandy whose son, Big James, was built like a giant but by temperament was a big softie. The chief, who treasured his family's reputation for manliness above all things, gave his son a terrible time.

On one occasion, after a cattle raid in the north, Big James and his father were guiding the stolen herd along the banks of the river when their

prize capture, a huge bull, broke away from the rest and plunged out of sight over the river bank. James was just quick enough to catch it by the horns and seems to have secured the beast when a great splash told his father that the bull had gone into the river.

"The soft grip of a baby!" bellowed the chief in digust. "If you had been your father's son you would have kept hold."

"I have," replied the boy meekly, as he threw the bull's horn at his fathers feet.

Generally the Atholl Fergussons were the wildest of their race – the other branches came much more quickly into contact with the Saxon concept of law and order. It was only natural therefore that the highland branch should have become royalists and then Jacobites whilst most of their southern cousins were servant Whigs and Covenanters, yet still the pull of the Fergusson name could cut across political barriers.

In 1745 to 1746 virtually the whole of the Dunfallandy clan were led by their chief and served with the Atholl men who fought so effectively under Lord George Murray at Prestonpans, Falkirk and Culloden. Dunfallandy himself, however, fell victim to Prince Charlie's fatal decision to leave a garrison at Carlisle, on the retreat north from Derby.

The town soon fell to Cumberland and mass executions began with the Fergusson chief's head destined for a quick end. But when he heard of the unfairness of the Jacobite trials, James Fergusson of Pitfour, an advocate and cousin of Dunfallandy, rushed south to defend the prisoners.

It soon became clear that many were being hanged for the mere fact that they wore tartan so Pitfour smuggled one of his own servants into prison and then confounded the court by producing conclusive proof that he had been at home in Aberdeen throughout the rebellion.

This so sobered the court that Fergusson of Dunfallandy and many others, who were undoubtedly guilty of high treason, escaped with short prison sentences.

Chapter three:

Execution and persecution

The most famous of all the Highland Fergussons paradoxically was not a man of action but a philosopher and historian – Adam Fergussons, now widely regarded as the founder of the modern science of sociology. He was a son of the manse who had been raised from a poor home by one of the Fergusson university scholarships. Adam was a fine scholar from an early age who found his first employment as a chaplain to the Black Watch. He showed that he had some of the family fighting spirit by seizing a dead man's sword in battle and leading a charge against the enemy.

These and other experiences of military and political life stood him in good stead when he came to write his history of civil society, a study of the contrast between the old feudal system into which he had been born, and the emerging industrial civilisation he had discovered in the Lowlands. This work made his reputation and he became a professor of moral philosophy at Edinburgh University where for 50 years he was one of the leading lights of the greatest period of Scottish letters.

Adam Smith and David Hume were personal friends and at his house in 1787 Robert Burns met the young Walter Scott. Later Fergusson's sons and daughters became Scott's closest friends and the novelist was often to return to the theme of the losses and the transition from the old to the new Scotland of which Fergusson has given one of the best summaries –

"We may, with good reason, congratulate our species on their having escaped from a state of barbarous disorder and violence into a state of domestic peace and regular policy."

Robert Fergusson of Aberdeenshire, turfed out from his living as a Presbyterian minister at the Restoration in 1660, lived a life of high intrigue and danger in London and on the Continent where he earned the nickname Fergusson the Plotter. Between 1679 and 1683 he was deeply involved in schemes to exclude and assassinate the Catholic heir to the throne, later James II. Fergusson was one of the few conspirators to escape execution and fled to Holland, returning in 1685 as chaplain to the Duke of Monmouth's ill-fated attempt to overthrow King James.

After this ended in failure, Fergusson was again one of the few to escape with their lives, much to the suspicion of his whig friends that he was a Jacobite double agent.

The only conclusion one can draw from this astonishing career which ended in abject poverty in 1714 is that Fergusson simply enjoyed plotting and was not very fussy about who he was plotting against!

His younger brother James, meanwhile, led a more consistent life as a soldier, first in the Cameronian regiment raised to oppose the Jacobite Rebellion of 1689, and later in the Continental armies, rising to the rank of General by the time of his death in 1705.

He was the first of a whole series of accomplished Fergusson soldiers who in the next 200 years came from all branches of the clan to win honours in the American, Indian, Napoleonic and world wars.

Another slightly less honourable military man was Black Jack Fergusson, the naval captain, who sailed round the western Hebrides in the summer of 1746 vainly pursuing Bonnie Prince Charlie but capturing amongst others Flora Macdonald and Lord Lovat.

Lovat's capture ended tragically on London's Tower Hill with a public beheading. The old Jacobite fox thought he had secured himself an island in Loch Morar, which is separated from the open sea by a small neck of land. Fergusson surprised Lovat by dragging a boat from his warship across this neck, forcing the 80-year-old fugitive to hide in a hollow tree from which, unfortunately, his huge belly could be seen protruding.

It is said that Fergusson cruelly kept Lovat in suspense by pretending not to notice him and hovered around the tree for a full half hour before pouncing.

A rather more heroic figure of the '45 was piper Donald Fergusson who served as a vounteer in the Jacobite Army of the Northeast during a skirmish on the bridge at Keith. Donald played where the action was fiercest and did not stop even when an attack by the Government troops forced him off the bridge and into the river. It was lucky he kept afloat while several of his companions drowned about him. Donald seems to have lived on this story for years afterwards, swearing that so long as he could inflate his pipes he would neither "dee nor drown!" This prediction proved true for he died in his eighties, on the afternoon of the first day he found the effort of his morning practise too much.

The son of James Fergusson of Pitfour who rescued the Jacobites at Carlisle, also a James, was an Aberdeenshire M.P. for 30 years and a celebrated character. Though known everywhere simply as The Member he was said to have spoken only once during his entire career in the

House, although accounts vary over what he said.

One story is that he simply rose to move a motion that the window in front of which he sat should be mended as the draught was causing him great discomfort. The other version is that after 25 years silence he rose to speak on some subject at which some opponent began to shout, 'here here', before Fergusson had said anything. "I'll be damned if you do," replied the irate Scotsman and sat down never to rise again.

Another Aberdeenshire Fergusson, James the Astronomer, was the son of a poor peasant who became a real lad o pairts. Despite having no formal education, he worked out the principles of mechanics after being astonished to see his father raise their cottage roof with a lever. Later, as a shepherd, he plotted a map of the heavens while lying out at night with his flock, using a device like an abacus to measure the relative positions of the stars. The local gentry were so impressed by this that they sent him to Edinburgh to study. Soon Fergusson was making a living by painting miniatures, another skill he had taught himself while building complicated astronomical machines in his spare time. He eventually sold one of these machines for a small fortune in London, which enabled him to give the course of lectures that made his reputation and won him his Royal Society Fellowship. He died in the castle in 1776.

Fame of a different kind came to Robert Fergusson, the poet hero of Burns who was born at Edinburgh in 1750. The Fergusson bursaries took him to St. Andrews University but his father's death forced him to return to Edinburgh where he took menial work in a law office to support his mother and sisters. His finest poetry reflected the humour and grim reality of street life in Auld Reekie.

Fergusson didn't keep good health and at the age of 21 fell victim to a brain fever from which he never recovered, dying in October 1774. His work inspired Burns so much that the Bard erected a headstone over Fergusson's pauper grave in the Canongate Kirkyard. In some famous lines he lamented the young poet's fate, blasting the gentry of Edinburgh for not buying his work, so denying a decent standard of living.

The Dumfriesshire and Ayrshire families were strong Covenanters and Whigs in the civil and religious troubles of the 17th and 18th centuries. The Whig triumph of 1688 ended 20 years persecution of the south western Covenanters, a period known as 'the Killing Times' by those who suffered under it.

Many tales have survived of the Fergusson exploits during these troubles when royal troopers roamed the moors of Ayrshire, Lanarkshire and Dumfries dispersing non-conformist prayer meetings and very often killing the participants.

On one occasion John Fergusson of near Monaive was returning from one of the outlawed convecticles. Seeing he was alone a soldier charged but Fergusson got a head start on him by nipping through a hole in the wall, which ran along the road. Then, in a chase reminiscent of Tam O'Shanter, he just managed to escape by leaping a stream, which the troopers' horses refused to cross.

Unfortunately Fergusson had to endure the full blast of a musket on his behind as he rose in the saddle to clear the stream. It was his last leap anywhere for several months!